LE(

DAVID HARSENT

Legion

faber and faber

First published in 2005
by Faber and Faber Limited
3 Queen Square London WC1N 3AU
Published in the United States by Faber and Faber Inc.
an affiliate of Farrar, Straus and Giroux LLC, New York.

Typeset by Faber and Faber Limited
Printed in England by T. J. International Ltd, Padstow, Cornwall

A CIP record for this book
is available from the British Library

ISBN 0-571-22809-7

2 4 6 8 10 9 7 5 3

i.m. Mary Dorothy May Harsent

Acknowledgements

Thanks to the editors of the following publications and organisations who first published, broadcast, or commissioned some of these poems: *Acumen, Agenda, London Review of Books, Modern Poetry in Translation, The North, The Poem, Poets Against the War, Times Literary Supplement, Vallum* (Canada), *The Wolf* and the Palace Theatre, Watford.

'The Woman and the Hare (1)' was commissioned by the Nash Ensemble and set to music by Harrison Birtwistle. It had its premiere at the South Bank Centre in March 1999 (soprano: Claron McFaddon; reciter: Julia Watson; conductor: Lionel Friend).

'Notes from Exile' was commissioned by BBC Radio 3's *Poetry at the Proms 2000*.

Stelae makes free use of passages from Worth's Dartmoor.

Special thanks to Alice Kavounas for literal versions of Yannis Ritsos.

Contents

II STELAE

III

I
LEGION

Despatches

shape of a man

broken legs, sit-dragging himself, knuckling the clay,

iron gates, beyond the

not quite the broad bright light of day,
no, but well past the dead of night. You couldn't say
much about any of that, the how or why.
Not broken legs, no, but something gone
in his back perhaps. You could see him guern
with effort, hunched, as he scraped along between
road and verge, between stone and fern,
until finally

not gates, no, in fact

proved a play
of the light; more a place where things just fell away

The Wall

A milky, dead-eye sky. That steel-and-cordite smell
you get with a lightning strike. Ripples underfoot. A
    taste
of nickel behind your tongue. The best and last
grouped on the far side, waiting to go to the wall,
their voices just a dim hubbub at first,
like something on the boil,
then raised in a sudden awkward cheer, then still.

Soon after which (we should have guessed)
the first hint of that unearthly weather: a test
of music in summer orchards, birdsong, a single bell
tolling at dusk over ploughland, over water-meadows:
    all
we have learned, at length, to mistrust.

You could hear it, low and visceral,
coming in off the skyline, airborne and moving fast.

Patrol

Rough ground, it seemed, as we rode through; but a last
glance revealed rows of sleepers clabbered in dust
that puckered and puffed as their dreams erupted,
each man cloaked and his weapon in his fist.

We pulled over, not sure what to do for the best.
This dead-to-the-world, this unity of breath,
wasn't what we'd expected,
children stock still in the shadows,
a rush-light behind the grille of the 'facility for widows'.

Crapshoot

Then everything closed down, the 'full systems
    malfunction'
we'd been told to expect; a blip in the light of the world
was more what it was: a trip-switch on creation.

Some took to their beds; some played wild
music, as if the thing might be kept off
by the sheer burst of it; some spiked jugs of juice
and called their children in; some yammered; some threw
    dice,
the bounce of the bones like a chuckle or a cough.

Barlock

'. . . you can't think,' she was saying, 'beyond the next.
We were underground, closed-out, we'd slammed the
 hatch,
the two of us, him wearing everything from his stickpin
 to his Rolex,
me dressed to kill. The first fast batch
showed as lights over the mountains. We barely had
 time to catch
our breath or point before they sewed a chainstitch
across Katchukama Square and down the Street of
 Locks.
That's when we went to the cellar: to cobwebs on bare
 bricks,
a tin trunk, a rusty Barlock, empty wine-racks,
pictures in busted frames, a doll's house, Meccano,
 Airfix,
all the old stuff, history in a box . . .

I had plaster in my hair that made my whole scalp itch,
he looked like hell, lip bitten-through, a raw patch
on the heel of his hand from hammering home the latch.
For an hour or more we could hear the phone and the
 fax
cross-ringing upstairs: that, and the chiming of clocks
with the incoming overlapping. I made a bed of sacks
and lay down with him, my hand tucked tight between
 his legs.
I dozed and dreamed of our place in the south, the
 beach,
the dunes and pines, the walk between rocks

that took us to the village, no more, really, than a few
    shacks,
a taxi rank, a bar, where he liked to hang out with the
    jocks, the jacks
of all trades, patriots, punks, argufiers, the one-time
    rich,
two-timers, time-servers: salt of the earth, he'd say. I
    said the dregs.'

Caterpillar

Our first snow of the winter came last night,
which is how we knew they'd gone through: cross-thread
tyre tracks, the Greek key-pattern of a caterpillar tread.

You wouldn't have seen them, topped off in white,
boots and all, vehicles draped in white, or painted white,
white facepaint too, the only part not white the white
of their eyes, and the long, slow column moving across a
    dead-
white landscape like a marble bas-relief. We prayed
after that, the village down on its knees in the slushy wet:
that they'd keep moving, that their purpose was fixed,
    that the raw
skies would fetch more snow, that no more need be said,
that first was last, that nothing might surface after the
    first spring thaw.

Daisychain

When we saw the smoke, we knew. The smoke was
    indelible.
Some went to the lowland scrub, some to the sacred
sites, but some (some women, I mean) found another
    way, hard,
as if a word had been spoken, as if it might be infallible,
as if, last night, it had come to them in dreams,
the blade going from hand to hand, each making the
    second cut
on the one before in case she couldn't, in case it came to
    that.
Others were ashamed and did what they did in private
coming to light later, some in the orchards, some from
    house-beams.

Well, they must have gone round us. We sent men out
next day and the day after that, but the world was
    empty, it seems;
of that smoke, not a trace; of that word, not a syllable.

Despatches

       moved, under darkness, from the high
ground to the water-meadows and the farmed fields near
the outskirts, then radio silence

       at first, or why
no birdsong, no distant music, no smoke on the clear

       but made our advance as per
and went through

               regrouped and came to a slow
stop in the Street of Songs

       deployed between row after row
of silent houses, fanning out, going low; but no one was there,
of course, just the household pets and a farcical clumsy
pig that took half a clip to stop. An after-smell of fear
round everything

       thrown hither and yon by the sheer

*and traces among the rubble, enough to give you the heebie-
jeebies, as you might imagine, and bad enough; but more
than that, the inside-out of bedsheets on the road, the lazy-
susan in a ditch, the chair drawn up to a fireplace, the stair
-way to nowhere, CDs, TVs, DVDs, PCs, VCRs*

fishslice; Dream Wedding Barbie

Toffee

There was a man who made toffee; he would leave it to
   cool
on a blue-veined marble slab by the open window
of his shop, which was little more than a tin-and-timber
   lean-to
in the Street of Songs. There was a man who made small
animals and the like – horses, mostly – from scraps of
   steel
the plough turned up: high-grade stuff he could fine-tool;
while he worked he would sing, as if he had someone to
   sing to.
There was a man who made paintings: portraits, as a rule,
of businessmen in their best; though he made one, once,
   of a fool
wearing a crown of stars and pissing a bright arc, while
   behind him
the Devil herded souls through a *vesica piscis*, its holy seal
ruptured. I thought that if I could find him,
or one of the other two, or any in that street, I might
   know
what became of my house and those in it; and what to
   do; and where to go.

Art

Before this, I liked a sketchiness in art,
figures, say three or four, half-done in white on almost-
    white,
or something much like a bruise
seeping up through the wash, so you might make out,
if you stood side-on to the thing, eye-hollows, a nose,
or a mouth saying O–O–O: whites, but also blues
deep enough to make mauve in moonlight or snowlight
(was it?) and these few standing still, standing apart,
but more at their backs, a hidden weight in the canvas.

It's everywhere, now, in the city's broken stone, in the
    glint
off smashed glass, in the much-told tale
of the bombed-out house where someone peeled off the
    wall
a face stuck flat that came away whole
still wearing the puckish stare of the hierophant,
just a touch or two left on the whitewash, the art of
    hint.

Snapshots (1)

Troopers dead in a trench and a river of rats

Topers dead in a bar and a flood of reflections

Lovers dead in bed and a shift of maggots

Snipers dead in the trees and a cowl of crows

Travellers dead on the bridge and a gaggle of gawpers

Oldsters dead on a porch and a downpour of flies

Deserters dead in a ditch and a raft of chiggers

Foragers dead in a field and a jostle of foxes

Children dead at their desks and a month of Sundays

Ghost Archaeology

We cut our engines, then, and the dust
settled in silence. Much later, everyone mentioned the
    same strong sense
of things siphoned-off, like a vacuum chasing a bomb-
    blast:
no birds, no beasts, no weather; and, inside the fence,
only a smudge in mud, a dint in the grass,
ash-and-clinker negatives, and everywhere the print
of hobnails. All bad enough, though the worst,
we agreed, was whatever-it-was, shiny and plump like a
    worm-cast,
curled tightly against itself, though you felt there was no
    defence
for the little blunt head in the heft of the little blunt fist.

Late in the day, we broke open the seals
on the doors of the admin block and fetched out the
    blads, the reels
of thirty-five mill, the buckram-bound ledgers . . . the data.
Such orthodoxies there, such wheels within wheels,
such a rich and full account of the dark desiderata.

We bivouacked beyond the wire a good mile out, where
    the last light falls
on the distant bridges and spires of Terra Damnata,
then shifts to flood the wetlands as terns and teals
descend on Lake Torpid, as a quarter-
moon shows its face, at last, to the ever-thickening water,
as someone walking the picket line shivers, perhaps, and
    feels
that rush of twilight wind like the flocking together of souls.

All Hallows

On that day we go to the graveyard with eggs and
     plaited bread,
with candy and candles, with bucket-brewed liquor,
and talk to each other, and talk to the long-time dead.
Which is how they found us, gathered there
in our suits and silks, the whole village, as if we'd been
     led
by a taste for death, yes, by a whiff of death in the air.

They must have been glad of a square
meal, given the distance they'd covered, given the hard
road they'd travelled; they must have been glad
of something to cut the dust, of a chance to rest,
what with the promise of bad
weather backing from the west, with an all too rare
sight of ourselves caught between prattle and prayer;
and they must have been pressed for time, given their
     speed
with rope and wheel, as they showed us St Stephen,
     St Eulalia,
St Nicomedes, St Kilian, St Catherine, St Euphemia,
     St Jude.

What to say but that the women cut their hair
next day and threw the tresses in the yard, and fetched
     blood
from their cheeks; what to say but that we tore
all pictures from the walls; what to say but that we wore
ashes and clay, that some of the men went back with
     food,
as before, to recover the lost, to leave the raven's share.

The Piss-pail

We were dug in, just light of an apple orchard. You got
a faint scent from the whin until the dew burned off, and
  bird-
song out of the branches, or else a bullet.
One went up for a look-see, then another, then a third
as the trickster in the tree got off a shot
and clipped, as if he'd meant to, the piss-pail that stood
on the lip of the trench, which rose in the air and flipped
  like a lucky bet
once, then again, to come down flush over the third
  man's head
who buckled and blacked out, thinking he'd been hit.

We laid him under a flag. Kyrie eleison, we sang,
Christi eleison, until the earthworks rang,
and he opened his eyes to a world of light
such as he'd never seen, the cryptic white-on-white
of clouds and sky, white of gunsmoke, white of the
  trench walls,
whites of our eyes as we knelt and called to bring him
  back,
of his wife's shift, her steady smile, the slack
of her breasts as she stooped to gather windfalls.

Despatches

camp after
a journey of three days or more, no food, almost no water,
during which the guards took real delight

on a concrete floor,
soon running with their own

down like dogs, father and daughter,
mother and son, or taken out to the block where

the report states, amid 'general laughter'

Chinese Whispers

They told us about the boy who disappeared
when the convoy went through. Search
as they might there was no sign until word
was sent of 'residue' between the wheel and the wheel-arch.

*

News arrived of the women who went mad,
who kicked-in the windows of every billet,
who ran shrieking through the Street of Locks, who shed
their semmits and stays to dance a *carcan* in the market.

*

This one's got legs: the man who went down to the river
under fire, searching among that day's dead for his only
 brother,
turning the bodies, one by one, to discover
his wife, son, uncles, sister, father, mother.

*

The Surgeon General, they say it was, who went back
to drink the last of his Roffignac, to sit in a dry bath
and open a vein: a man, for sure, on the right track.
One for the road. One for the primrose path.

*

Hardly a day goes by but someone boasts
of having been there when those men downed weapons
with barely a word, and walked through their own lines,
later reported as slips of the tongue, or ghosts.

*

How's this for a tale of slaughter:
a man who slew his herd, then drew a hood
over the trembling head of each blonde daughter
and shot them where they stood?

    *

Word of mouth has a gut-shot man walk all of ten
miles from the front to his own front-door, lift the latch,
find them dead, dig seven graves, fire the thatch,
fill his bottle, sling his gun, walk back again.

    *

Here's one about the raw recruit who crawled out from
   beneath
the corpses of his comrades, like a dinner guest
emerging from a bun-fight scrum, to charge the
   machine-gun nest
armed with only a shovel, with only a trowel, with only
   a toothpick, with only his teeth.

Duet

When they opened up, smoke played out like a banner:
their true colours. We cut loose with the heavy stuff,
working blind, spot-grouping on a whim
until it cleared and we saw them going down. Don't
   laugh,
but I found myself singing along with the old Maxim-
Nordenfelt's bass-baritone 'hosannah, hosannah,
   hosannah!'

Honey

With word getting back to us of a very real chance
of pestilence by day and pestilence
by night, the father would go 'on forays' to the ring-
    fence,
small-talking the guards, checking on how things stood
for anyone making a break for the open road.

The mother braided her hair and laid in food:
he was the pioneer, she was the goodwife,
him with his father's rook-gun, her with her mother's
    recipe
for hunter's stew, with her flour and yeast, with her
    longlife
milk, with rice, with wrasse, with huss, beef jerky,
    turkey,
lemons, lemon curd, cured ham, lamb both on and off
the bone, pizza, pesto, pasta, tabouleh, flageolet
beans, beans both baked and green, green
tomatoes, sprats in brine, Cheddar, Cheshire, the locally-
    grown
cabbage and kale, salt beef, salt pork, Saltines, salt
both sea- and Cerebos, apples, apricots, biscuits, brisket,
    brawn . . .

Each day more of the same, with no one to call a halt:
his honeyed words to the wide-eyed sentries,
her shelf on shelf of honey, the 'product of many
    countries'.

Filofax

The entire township, heading north in cars, in trucks, on
    bikes, on foot,
some with next to nothing, some choosing to cart
(as it might be) armchair, armoire, samovar, black and
    white
TV, toaster, Filofax, Magimix, ladle, spindle, spinet,
bed and bedding, basin and basinette,
passed (each in clear sight) lynx and wolverine and bob-
    cat,
heading south to the guns and the promise of fresh
    meat.

Street Scenes

(i)

Two greybeards playing chess, would you believe,
their sweetwood table and chairs at one remove
from the corner of the crossroads, where a dove
drifts down through the trompe l'oeil clouds of a gable-
   end to LOVE
IS ALL YOU NEED and SNAJPER! One grips his sleeve
to wipe his nose; one threatens the knight's move.
The same crossroads where push has so often come to
   shove.

(ii)

Broken glass in the Street of Clocks
Empty coats in the Street of Spindles
In the Street of Bridegrooms, broken locks
Burning books in the Street of Candles

(iii)

If you look closely you can see what it is, but you do
   have to look
closely, what with the early-evening light skating on the
   slick
and coming back at you off puddles on the tarmac.
This would have been three hours or more after the
   attack,
everything lying heavy, everything seeming to own the
   trick
of stillness, that shopping trolley, for instance, the gutted
   truck,
and these: one face-down over there, one in the crook

of another's arm, one flat out, one heaped like an open
    book,
one caught on the turn, arms out like a stopped clock,
one leaning against a door, as if about to knock.
But that over there: look again: did you ever see the like?

(iv)
The 'Golden Couple of Ballroom' are dancing the alley-
    ways,
soft-shoeing amid the shrapnel, lost in each other's gaze.

(v)
Something going through, something much like a hound
or wolf, in the hour *entre chien et loup*, the blue
hour when birdsong stops, just for a minute or two,
and the dead in the graveyard shuffle up the queue.

Something lean and low-slung, its muzzle to the ground,
something leaving a drip-trail of blood or piss.
It has come by way of the rift and the pretty pass,
slipping between the dead cert and the near-miss.

Something that whines and whimpers, much like the
    sound
of a child in pain, or love's last gasp. It shows
a backbone like a hat-rack, an eye like a bruise,
in its mouth, a rib (is it?), dark meat, the pope's nose.

Mascot

Out of the mess of flags, out of the slit-trench,
out of the field of hands, out of the carpet of hair,
out of the roll of smoke, out of the right royal stench,
out of the missed chance, out of the bad hunch,
comes the rat with his madcap stare.

Out of the pup tent, out of GCHQ,
out of the pill-box, out of the sniper's lair,
out of the British square, out of the last of the few,
out of the the least part, out of a hole in the heart, out of
    the blue,
comes the rat with the rat's share.

Despatches

stop at nothing, think nothing of

nothing more, nothing less

like nothing on God's earth

so nothing for it, but to

could do nothing, unless

*all went for nothing, so we rigged the trucks
leaving nothing that might anger or betray, and then made tracks
for the lowland swamps, where nothing could follow. Such treks,
of course, are nothing to seasoned men, though one or two tricks
learned from the locals were nothing if not*

was all and nothing else

nothing to say

where nothing remained, nothing more
to be seen, nothing more to be heard, nothing on two legs,
nothing on four, nothing, in fact, but

Harp Strings

(i)

Then we had iron rain, nine days without break or let, the
    rain
that is nothing more nor less than rain of the season
spilling into our songs as 'fist of nails' or 'harp strings'
or 'love of solitude'. Should we have guessed they would
    gain
ground under that cover? Well, look, the reason
we turned to our bottling and sewing, to pot-luck and
    make-good,
is simple enough to tell: the rain only ever brings
music in mist or sweet bafflement or rain-dreams. There's a
    birch-wood
on the outskirts, silver poles no thicker than a man, where
    the rain swings
and shudders, wind-blown walking rain, and their top-to-
    toe
silver-grey, and the steel of their sidearms, and bone-
ash mixed with clay slapped to their cheeks and necks is how
they came among us, backed by the wind, the stain
of their last battle carried like a blazon on the brow.

(ii)

The rain washed everything, took everything downhill, a
    log-jam,
a slurry, that side-slipped to the river. White water rang
on broken boulders and roared in the mid-stream slam,
then it all went clear. We've owned to it since; we were
    wrong
to see nothing dark in the rain. All this has gone into song.

Cairn

(This was before.) A cairn had been raised close to a tree
    that fruits
so its blossom would sweeten the stone. (Before things
    were broken and taken.)
Men would climb to the place in dog-light, some with a
    token
pebble, some with a punnet of ash, some in their wed-
    ding suits.

Sniper

I am tucked up here out of sight. I am tucked up here
in the bell-tower of Our Lady of Retribution: my own
   space
well-stocked and arranged just so. This tower was raised
   in the year
blank-blank, the year of the crow, the year of our disgrace.
I am tucked up here in the shadow of the cross
with my ear-muffs, with my quilt and palliasse,
kneeling up but looking down, like a man at prayer.

A woman carrying water crosses the square.
She is running slowly, running not to spill. Then a child,
   out into clear
view, going a long diagonal and running like a hare,
jink-jink. I am tucked up here, a sure thing, with my
   sausage and beer
and a field-stove to keep my fingers supple. Days pass.
I'm more than content in my snuggery, my lair;
I have somewhere to lay my head and somewhere to piss
and, for comic disputation, the birds of the air.

With the scope pulled up to my eye, the world is close
and particular: this grandad, hugging the shade, each
   hair
on his head, the wet of his eye, the pre-war
coin on his fob-chain, the weave of his coat . . . Over
   there
by my friend the Marlboro Man is where
I would sit with my morning coffee: Arno's place,
its pinball machine, its jukebox, the girl with Madonna's
   face

until she showed her teeth; I would tilt my chair
to the wall and take the sun. They go in fear. They go in
  fear
of me. And where they go they go by my good grace.

I am tucked up here with plenty left in store.
The night-sky floods then clears, flagging a single star,
and the city settles to silence under my peace.
The woman, the child, the grandad, are nothing . . . or
  nothing more
than what history can ignore, or love erase.

Finisterre

That slim isthmus where one sea beats on the southern
    shore,
another sea on the northern, is called by sailors and
    strangers Finisterre
or, sometimes, Terra Nada. It was there,
on that cold strip of rock and broom and bright rag-
    weed that four
hundred were run to ground,
motherless sons, widowers, the orphans of orphans, their
    gear
tossed on the tide or lost to the offshore wind.

So much for gyromancy, so much for prayer.

We went there next morning, the weather holding clear,
and made a ring, the faint-hearted hand-in-glove with
    the blind.
It wasn't long before one of the women claimed to hear
a difference in the gulls' cries, something raw,
full-throated, a note so thick with fear
it took her breath and brought her to her knees. The air
was full of it then – everyone heard it clear,
or said they did, and stood in awe
to be there as the legend rose and formed,
the skirl of the dead in our ears, their silt still on the
    sand.

Snapshots (2)

A damsel in trouble with something too heavy to haul

Somebody stealing a morsel that somebody stole

A man with a rifle caught between stumble and stall

The mythical hole in the equally mythical Bible

Lost in the litter, a bauble or fol-de-rol

Line after line of them just about able to hobble

Tracer-shells lifting the lid off the Metropole

A string-quartet bowing amid the rubble

Squaddies drawn round in a ring to shuffle and deal

A shrapnel-wound pursing its lips and blowing a bubble

Swept up with the rest a nose-bone a shin-bone an eye-
ball

Cup and platter and spoon and potato-peel

The Goodwife's Tale

They touched her they didn't touch me. I wasn't
   touched.
The neighbour her recipe for Lenten cake they touched

her they didn't touch me. I wasn't touched. The teacher
her way with words they touched her

they didn't touch me. The girl from *Paris Chic* her switch-
switch walk they touched

her they didn't touch me. I wasn't touched.
The seamstress her stitch

in time they touched her they didn't touch me. The
   torch-
singer her Cry Me a River they touched

her they didn't touch me. The stenographer her touch-
typing they touched

her they didn't touch me. I wasn't touched. The doctor
   her catch
as catch can they touched her they didn't touch

me. My mother my aunt my sister-in-law my sister my
   daughter
-in-law they touched my daughter

they didn't touch
me my blonde my crowning glory. I wasn't touched.

Arena

Not everything dead is buried in that place
of rapid shadows. They're all in place, some head-

to-tail or arse-up, some cheek-by-jowl or face
to face (whether or not they were married), some in
   place

of others who say there's nothing to be said
and turn the earth at night and know their place.

The markers are blank, since everything's taken as read
in a place like that. Not everything buried is dead.

Despatches

[06:00hrs]

> *as per, and just at daybreak pulled*
> *out, sun and moon both high, the dawn wind cold,*
> *our long silhouette unfolding as we rolled*
> *downhill towards the final*

[08:00hrs]

> *ever-present danger of friendly*

[09:00hrs]

> *Songs, the Street of Locks, everything under a low*
> *ceiling of smoke, but no sign of life, no sound except a radio*
> *we couldn't get a fix on, but coming from somewhere below*
> *ground it seemed, as if the entire*

[09:45hrs]

picked up the broadcast. We heard
the news and the news was us, then music, classical, weird
getting that stuff out here

toccata

[11:00hrs]

or Bach or

II

STELAE

'Black' may derive from two very different sources, either 'bleak' or 'black', both of which come from the A-S 'blaec' meaning pale or colourless. He insists on 'bleak'. If we take the first meaning, the limit of paleness is white, and places bleak and exposed are apt to be covered with snow, as on the day of his birth. The other extreme of colourlessness is black and this colour also suits him well enough. The task of determining which meaning of black is intended is wellnigh hopeless, so many places are called both black and bleak, cold rain on a clitterfield, crows on a fallen ewe, who shall say just what he had in mind?

Rowe says that but twenty stones were standing, several having fallen. A maid in want of a man must walk the row and come into the circle, thinking of her choice: so will it be granted. Croker, writing three years later, says that twenty-seven stones formed the circle, of which several were prostrate. A barren woman should walk the round, going against the sun, then attend her husband that night: so will her child take root. Ormerod states that twenty-nine stones were erect, and two prostrate. Bring to the circle a child in sweat and pass the infant thus from hand to hand: so will the fever break. Murray sets the tale at twenty-six standing stones and six fallen. This was the third year of the war, and deep winter. Chudleigh reports twenty-three stones as standing, but does not say how many lay fallen. All these things are true as stated.

One writer insists, 'That occupants of the moor used divination by the crystal is shown by clear quartz prisms having been discovered tolerably frequently.' In truth, no more have occurred than can be fully accounted for by those naturally present in the soil, apart from the finger-length in his mother's sewing-box, given her by Mother Dark. Our bold historian continues thus: 'That they loved to play at games is shown by the numbers of little round pebbles, carefully selected, some for their bright colours, that have been found on the floors of the huts.' This is in error; the number of 'little round pebbles' which have been found is quite insignificant, and the proportion of those found which were 'brightly coloured' is trivial; possibly three such have come to light, lost near Becka Brook, to his great sorrow, when the whole bag spilled out, his best snake corkscrew, moonie corkscrew, milky oxbloods, turkey-heads, cats' eyes, flaming dragon, orange wasp and peewee.

It is obvious that Dartmoor granite does not yield readily to the weather. However, it is quite possible in the darkest of foggy nights to determine the points of the compass; and this by noting the face on which the rock has been most deeply incised by the weather. A man in drink who might be otherwise quite without hope might note that this face will be approximately towards the south-south-west, the direction of the prevailing and wettest wind. By this means he might make his way back or onward, whichever seems the wiser course. As a rule, the coarse-grained will yield more readily.

But in the sense of 'clear; eminent'. And, indeed, this is a characteristic to be noted in such an obvious and elevated landmark or rendezvous, where one might say, 'I'll see you by Hel'; or 'Come by Hel.' A second, notable, occurrence here is pseudo-bedding, most likely the result of a distinct and protracted cooling (his dry laugh) though opinion on this issue is divided and a few marked coincidences might lead to hasty generalisation. In this manner (his wry smile) it is easy to fall into ready error.

Here a kist is set on
an earth-fast boul-
der, which supplies
a floor. It is more
usual, however, that
the floor of a kist-
vaen should be the
bare subsoil and the
side and end stones
set in this, the top-
soil or 'meat earth'
being on the out-
side, the cover-stone
above the surface
and, over all, a bar-
row or cairn, which
sometimes might be
domed. Meat earth,
they said; he imag-
ined the spade-cut,
the   welling-up.
When opened, the
kist was found to
have been refilled
with subsoil mat-
erial   containing
some charcoal and
a little bone ash.
Meat and bone and
ash. He misread
domed as doomed.

This fine stone
remotely   placed
in wild surround-
ings, brings little
back   to   mind
except, as with all
these,   the   wind
hanging on gran-
ite   edges   and
singing its song.
Likewise,   the
Hanging Stone or
Leaning   Rock
(which   seems   a
genuine   menhir
of   prehistoric
date) hands noth-
ing down except,
as he would have
it, the wind hang-
ing   on   granite
edges and singing
its   death-song.

A fine kistvaen was unearthed in the centre of a sepulchral circle and therein were found two coils of human hair. This was close to his birthplace. While no traces of carnal interment have been found in any mound-covered kistvaen, there is nothing to render inhumation impossible, as he himself points out. A chest two feet six inches to three feet in length by two feet in width and depth is normally ample for contracted interment. He offers the notion of pitch pine or wicker, in order to avoid the use of unsustainable hardwoods. That cremation was widely practised by barrow builders is very certain. This he enters as a fine alternative. The strongest and most reliable evidence of cremation is burnt bone: burnt human bone being certain evidence, that and the moon rising red, a flayed hare on the evening of the very day.

III

The Woman and the Hare (1)

To Harrison Birtwistle

I have come to this place to be shot of myself, I have
    come to come
to nothing, or less than nothing if nothing
is absence and absence nothing more than a face or
    name
gone missing. Yes, even less. Worse off than without.
Moonshine makes this lush landscape a washout.

*

I saw a hare standing in standing corn
and another hare couched in the seas of the moon.

*

I have come to this house in grey-green weather,
this empty house with its delicate corpses of crane-fly
    and spider,
I have come to come to nothing. My breath
would scarcely ruffle the dust or turn a feather.

*

Today, there is rainfall across the setting sun.
The long fields seem to burn
and drown, rendering down the last of feather and bone.

*

A day, a month . . . it's part of the same long fever.
They are reaping the last of the corn. The hare breaks
    cover.

*

Now she lies up in stubble. Now she goes to ground
in bracken, where men set fires to catch the crosswind.
I shall do less and less. Each morning
will find me less myself, less than next to nothing.
Now she cuts a mad caper, her body a taper, yes, her
    body burning.

                *

I burn. I am winnowed to a wick.
Almost completely shot of myself. Cut back to the quick.
The moon looms heavy and red over a field of stooks.

                *

Her flesh falls from the bone. The worst has gone
to the fire, the rest is mine.
She is changed, she is all but meat.
Cut and come again. I lift my hand and eat.

At the Graveside

Here at the midwinter graveside you are what they
      might call 'drop-
dead gorgeous' – aren't you? – with your toning greys
      and blacks,
your kitten heels, your snappy hat with its crop
of . . . nightshade, is it? Who but you could make the
      vicar hop
and skip beside the bier to catch you up?
Who but you, standing aside to weep
while the younger mourners bunch and crane their necks?

What if this whole business should suddenly hum to a
      stop
in a series of faltering frames, each of us frozen in step,
the bearers bent by the dead weight on their backs,
rain teased out by the wind, a pall of rooks
tumbling into stillness round the spire?
What if we found ourselves locked-off and everything
      hang-fire?
Would you stay young? Would you keep your looks
in a place like that, where only the dead may sleep?

I think you are thinking hic jacet which brings me round
      to sex
on a catafalque, underscored by the curl and slap
of the churchyard firs. Maybe you'll let me cop
a feel at the wake, or suffer me to slip
into the bathroom when you take out your gear and
      touch up
your face. Why does so much have to depend on *Perhaps*,
or how fast I can get my fist round a bottle of Becks?

I seem to have you in close-up now, every raindrop
that blurs your eye, that hangs in your hair, that clings
    so to your lip.
What are you staring at? Can you see all the way to the
    bluestone rocks
of our home-from-home on the coast? Are you wonder-
    ing how it would be
to drive all night, to arrive, to bed down, to wake up
on a morning of sun and gulls, my dead weight on your
    back,
to shrug me off, then rise for your first sight of the sea?

By Sennen

After a painting by Jeremy LeGrice

. . . in London, of course you are, landlocked
in your kitchen, but just a step, after all,
from the door into the hall, and then just a step
from the door into the street
where the cabbie is more than happy to wait
by the slip-road that takes you out through the wrecked
hulks of tower blocks, happy to stop-
start-stop in the backed-
up traffic, its tide-race of tail lights,
its surf of crap and slop,
letting you out with a minute or so to spare
for the westbound train, a minute
or less, so you scarcely believe you've done it,
except landing-lights in the bare
backs of houses are slipping past
too fast for counting, while some sudden, clear,
cold wind is shaking the fire-escapes
like rigging, and that sky-high blur
of dark cloud laid on darkness is the test
of where you are, of what you'll come to next,
which is why you fall asleep from fear or habit,
which is why you wake up with the ghost
of kitchen-whiskey, why the first and last
shreds of memory hold only the best and worst
of what you first intended, as your fist
strikes the window, as your foot
slaps the platform, putting you just a step, a step
or two, from the cliff path and the path
that goes from the cliff to the beach,
wind ringing your ears almost as much

as the cries of seabirds which fast
become the birds themselves, afloat
on the massive uprush of air that flows from the root
of the cliff and up over its lip, which makes you think,
'*Bird's-eye view: myself just pate and boot
and little salt-white hands,*' while you trample out the
    pith
and bladder of seaweed, setting off the unholy stink
from its silky, liverish reds, beyond which
lies nothing, lies nothing at all, unless
it's the sea that cheats the eye, the sea that gives endless
accounts of itself, running green and green-and-white,
and a deeper green beneath; you can hear it, can't you,
that low-in-the-throat, that hysterical hiss;
you keep your eye on the fault-line, don't you,
where sea and sky squeeze out a line of light;
you'll stay there, won't you,
fronting the weather, learning it all by rote? –
'*Bird's-eye view: myself almost out of sight,
little salt-white . . .*'

And that deeper green beneath to prompt you.

At the Riverside

Watching this flow past and fall away into darkness
I think of when that mad old woman told me her life had
   been
'a waste of time' (by which she meant a year-in, year-out loss)
as she stared me down, her yellow corpse-hair, corpse-
   rouge, corpse-
breath, the whole of herself bitten back to the bone.

Just here, the river goes brown-to-grey-to-green.
The towpath is wild garlic, hawthorn, leafmould, dogshit,
   dross
of night-time reckonings, the broken iron
of fence posts and mooring posts, black ash of last night's
   fires
where the lowest of the low communed with the unclean . . .

She might be one of them. These days she might dress
only in sacking and newsprint, drink only rainwater, eat
   only grass,
might be that halfway Holy Fool who's sometimes seen
preaching in Oxford Street, bending and baring her skinny
   arse
to the tourists, the shoppers, the cops, the monuments to
   commerce,

might be found, for all I know, among the elegant insane
who quickstep the London pavements, dancing to bring on
   chaos,
but mostly get wrong-footed and bring on rain,
who come to the roadside shrine of Our Lady Who Feels
   No Pain
with their sacrament of bin-food and cider cut with meths.

It's all but dark. Bats pick off the bright-eyed moths,
the fox nips up the shrew, the rat sniffs out the nest;
    slayer and slain
finding each other in joy. '. . . and why such fuss,'
she continued, 'about who we are or what we might
    have been
if it comes to this: cracked laughter, the world as
    shadow, nil by mouth?'

Notes from Exile

This is my sixteenth week on Cape Terrablanche,
well dug in. Dug in and out of touch.
I am much taken up with this and that; with such and such.

    *

My voice and the wind are one and the same, same as that
    white
bird cruising above the snowfield. Not easy to say what's
    what.
Not easy in a place of endless light.

    *

My sixteenth week, I think. No telling day from night, no
    telling
minute from minute. It is snowing, now, because it is
    always snowing.
White laid on white is endlessly revealing.

    *

Colour comes in dreams; in dreams I lapse
into blues that are more than just the way snowlight strikes
    ice,
more than the blue of fingernails or lips.

    *

No sun, not ever, and no moon either; to look long at the
    sky
is to grow a cataract. White above and white below,
myself between. It will snow more by and by.

    *

A cairn of snowballs on a plinth of ice. I am making my
　　mark.
This and that . . . such and such . . . reflections on the meek
and their just desert. If I stop to listen, I can hear myself
　　speak.

　　　＊

Yesterday, walking my round, I thought I saw
a figure coming towards me, stepping out in the raw.
It was snow whipped up by the wind. Yesterday, or the day
　　before.

　　　＊

Night is when I sleep, that's how I know.
If not dreams of colour, or dreams of voices, then dreams
　　of snow
and footprints doing dance steps: heel and toe, heel and toe.

　　　＊

Geometric whites: a disc, a rhombus . . . modernist
flim-flam. Today, I made two snowmen, each man fully
　　dressed
in snow, one with his back turned, one with a raised fist.

　　　＊

You can always hear the wind; that and the sound of ice
grinding ice, or ice splitting, or pitching into the sea some
　　place
north of here. It sounds north. And deeper yet, the tide-race.

At the Roadside

If I pull over just here, I'm a hundred miles from you
and a hundred miles from the place I'm going to,
up on the hard shoulder with the artics slamming past
on one side, on the other a field of barley or some such,
the roadside row bearing a hard dark crust
of crud, bearing also the stench
of diesel and oestrus: nose-to-tail trucks, creatures nose to
      tail
who might be the last of their species, hunting the night-
      spill
for food and each other, all their instinct and guile
come down, in these final days, to fuck and kill.

The wide black skidtrack snaking into the scrub,
the chunk of tyre with its inch-deep cleats,
a fan of feathers, a fist of claws, the blind O of a hub-
cap . . . Hieroglyphs of terra incognita. Count the beats
of the slow-lane slipstream: you seem to get the bass
blur of the theme from that film where he's out of rehab
and driving home, when he catches the neon splash
of a sky-high logo featuring the ace
of spades, whereupon he pulls over at once and starts a tab
he knows he can never back with cash.

Folie circulaire, you said; *love or, leastways, love-and-hate . . .*

Sun-and-cloud, side winds, rainfall; the trick is to sit tight
and the weather will come to you along that ten-county
      strip,
yourself a slim silhouette, the radio growing faint,
your breath misting the windscreen, and a hint
of something sour mixed in with your body heat

. . . or mine, as it happens . . . while the last airwave lets
   slip
news of the planet rendering down to crap.

I could read the owner's manual. I could clock-watch. I
   could sleep.
I could walk at dusk through the hip-
high barley, or whatever it is, and come to the Travel
   Lodge
by way of a farther field, by way of a hawthorn hedge,
by way of the car park, by way of the wheelie bins and
   air-
conditioning units, and take a room and go down to the
   bar
my purpose, of course, to pick up the Playtex rep,
already half-cut, to catch her eye, to catch her on the
   hop,
to pin her down with a heartfelt pledge
that will turn on the verb 'to cherish', to watch her drop
everything, down to the fluffy red *cache-sexe*
she filched from stock . . . And at three a.m. to get up
and find my way back in the dark with only a slop
of lights for guidance, which could be the lights of
   wrecks
out there on the strip, or that self-same line of trucks
shining blind as they barrel down the blacktop.

The Player

Here I am – take it on trust – behind my mask.
I will give it all from back here since it's what you ask.
This day-in, day-out stuff might look simple enough
but trip just once and everything's stutter and risk.

I find myself up against this seamless backcloth,
dyed in the wool, which depicts the eternal flow
of human affairs in the round and blow by blow:
it's easy enough to pick out *Wrath*

with his barbell pecs and the great gold disc
of the sun at his back and his hands to the wrist in
    blood;
and there's little *Rapine*, his anxious stare,
and *Love* (once *Rapture*) withdrawn in a white hood.

I am fully made up. Isn't this
the version of me that some version of you most desires?
Don't you fancy it more than that old-style hit-and-
    miss?
It comes with the sound-effect of a thousand-thousand
    choirs.

I can taste my own breath in here. I can feel
the sting of a tear that won't fall, which takes me right
    back
to the start and beyond, the last step, the real
thing, the one and only ecstatic dissolve-to-black.

There's *Guilt* at the lost-luggage window, there's *Hope*
ankle-deep, there's *Filth* with his soft soap,
there's *Fortune* with his one good eye. This is a story
you'll only get piecemeal. There's *Lust* in all his glory.

I never really loved you, and that's the truth.
I never loved anyone: I tried but missed by a mile.
Couldn't you hear the subtext in my laugh?
Couldn't you see the full set of teeth in my smile?

I stand here naked except for a trick of the light.
This second face is more my own
than the face I keep under repair and hidden from sight.
Can't you see who I am? Why, I'm yours and yours
    alone.

Applause, if you please, for the angels on their pin.
Applause for the psychopath on skates.
There's *Shame* in disguise. I'm growing a second skin
which seems to fit quite well. There's *Death* with all his
    mates.

And applause, of course, for the mummers and the
    mutes
who thrilled you with all you failed to understand.
You and yours will take to the street now; I remain,
my empty heart in my utterly empty hand.

At the Bedside

A chill in the nerve, an ache in the bone, enough
to bring anyone to bed . . . where she lies
sweating her own stain into the ticking, her final shape
    and size.
That cry is a slip of the tongue; that cough is off the cuff.

How on earth did I come here? Not by the snow-fields,
    not by
the parched arroyos of the south, not by the desert
    tracks
with their fragile lilac cacti, their lilac skies, their shy
rock-mice, their iguanas and sidewinders and hawks.
I remember the night-train, the distant fires, the deeper
    blacks
against the fieldscapes and the cloudwrack,
the girls who were happy to talk
for a while, then would turn or half-turn their backs
and settle to sleep, leaving me high and dry.

I have taken the bedside seat of the bleak executor,
though it's not my place, let me tell you, and not my
    burden.
She is murmuring something. If I look over her shoulder,
all at once it's first light in the garden –
blue light, the birch bole luminous, a fox
nose down, then making a sudden
leap-and-hop in the long grass by the midden
to snap up the little squealers and break their backs

– beyond which I can see the river, slow green glass,
and beyond that the city stew, a dim
skyline of steel and stone in a mist of fallout

and beyond that the high, bright skim
of the world itself, a meniscus of sea and sky
where the sorrows of earth and the sorrows of heaven
    meet,
and beyond that the dancing particles of space,
the atoms of dead stars, which is all she is
and ever was and all she will become.

In this long business there ought to be a clock
chiming into silence, then nightfall and the dead air,
things closing down as the window slowly darkens
and I look closer to find them there,
those girls with their thin-faced Slavic looks,
travelling towards a border that still beckons
despite the smudge of smoke, despite the lines of fire,
who smile, or seem to smile, who like to talk
but weary soon and turn to their own reflections,
and set themselves softly, sadly, cheek to cheek.

Tristichs

After Yannis Ritsos

A hallway of doors. A grandfather clock.
The woman came out naked, her hair wrapped in a
    towel.
She didn't look at the clock. It wasn't that.

*

Lemons hanging in mist make tiny lanterns.
Two horses are fetched, a grey and a strawberry roan.
You take the grey. The roan will be the death of me.

*

An insect on the window-pane, a burnt
match by the bedroom door:
something, or nothing at all?

*

I will bring this poem to an end
with an eyelash on your cheek
or a butterfly snarled in your hair.

*

It's hot. Clothes dry on balconies.
And, yes, here's the old woman in black.
The sun blanks her glasses.

*

Stone angels among broken columns
exchange kisses
over the graves of the long-since dead.

*

You passed me a glass of water
into which you had secretly
dipped your finger.

*

A train passing a village
late one Saturday. Indigo smoke.
A lone traveller.

*

They fed him honey, wine and cheese. They took him
to the arcades. In the Hall of Mirrors he saw
the young god, naked, his boots laced with gold.

*

Look – the new moon has just
slipped
a knife into her sleeve.

*

Pi-dogs. Dusty trees. A broken
balcony. A door into the night.
I have set my foot on the stairway.

*

She drops her bouquet on the bed.
She combs out her hair.
She strips off and goes to the window.

*

Each night, as you close your eyes, the unnameable
stands naked by your bed. It gazes
down at you and tells you everything.

*

With mother gone he makes his own coffee, he makes
his own bed. He's doing fine. His hands
have grown large, like mother's.

*

The sun finally reaches the backroom window.
Someone shouts outside in the street.
These things seem different to the loveless.

*

Black this side and white the other.
Your task – to make it
white this side and black the other.

*

Leaves step lightly on the nightwind;
in my sleep I hear them
and follow down to the taproot.

*

Imagine the restaurant, halogen-bright, the clash
of voices, the clash of dishes. Then silence as she
removes her shoes. As she begins to dance.

*

The station at night: silent, dark, deserted.
The station-master lights a cigarette.
He unzips and pisses down onto the tracks.

*

A closed house. A staircase.
A goldfish swims
in the tarnished mirror.

*

Your dress still pegged on the line.
A breeze fills it.
Suddenly, evening's here.

*

The smell of cooking from my neighbour's window.
At another window entirely, a man alone.
If I could hear her flute again, just once . . .

*

The entire city reflected
in your emerald ring:
my little house on the outskirts.

*

I flipped my cigarette-butt out of the window
into the cistern. Is it still glowing
or is that a shooting star?

*

He climbed the tower to toll the bell.
A bird looked him straight in the eye.
He sat down, then, and lit a cigarette.

*

The roses on your piano
shed a petal with each note you play.
Is that my fault? Is it?

*

Your sleep – a quiet lake.
A deer stoops to drink. I stoop
to drink.

*

What if these stones
fall into the sea? What if someone builds
a stone monument at the sea's edge?

*

When the shadow of a bird
falls on the white wall opposite,
I'll write you that letter.

*

She upturned the coffee cup.
'I see a door into the future.'
Open or closed? She didn't say.

*

The windows shuttered, the house empty apart
from the sleek and naked
absence of your body on the bed.

*

Those starlit nights . . . You could hear the apples
falling into the damp grass.
We let the apples lie, but gathered up the sound.

At the Quayside

If I raise my hand to wave, I'll never see you again:
that's the way bad luck goes, it works against the grain,
it limps up from behind, it knows you like its own,
has fifty different names for pain,
and so on and so on.

Your smile is custom-built, held ready, pearly-perfect.
Can you see me from there? I'm over here by the ticket-
office, side by side by side with the usual suspects.
Now the sun is playing morse on your locket
and I'm one of a cargo-cult.

Have you been down to steerage, are they truly
    beguiled?
Did the captain kiss your hand? Did the self-styled
Principe d'ella Conte ask if he might make so bold?
You told me blind faith would be your shield:
I believe you; believe me, I'm sold.

And now, as you set sail for the outer edge of the world,
a nation changes hands, markets overload,
they find the body of the missing child,
small wars ignite, blood talks to blood,
the bad tops out the good.

I see myself (don't you?) as the day wears on, still here;
the skyline closing down, the moon a blank stare,
the Outside Inn, the Greyhound, Rita's Bar
beginning to hum, opening their doors
to the shipping clerks and the whores.

And if she's not going home with him, I could go home
    with her,
as I did, or so I seem to remember, once before
and finally slept and woke on some broken shore
in a litter of jetsam rubbed raw
by the ocean's wear and tear.

The Woman and the Hare (2)

At three a.m. there are lights in the high-rise windows,
there are six-wheeler trucks hammering by on the slip-
　　roads,
there are people you don't want to meet in the back-
　　streets and side-streets.
The city never sleeps; or else it sleeps
like the hare, the fabled hare, with open eyes

> *eyes open, it's a dream*
> *eyes closed, it's a vision:*
> *the river splitting its seam*

It seems I can make what I will of clouds and the
　　nightwind:
the hare in a hood with the moon in her hand

> *hand in hand*
> *the insomniacs and the crooks*
> *each to his end*

End to end, the avenues fill with water,
with water or else with moonlight, it's tough to tell
with so bright a backwash, from this high angle.
I have come to the very end of ever after

> *after everything, this steady, slow*
> *unstoppable water, nowhere*
> *to be, nowhere to go*

Go down to the dormitory doorways, to the all-night
　　cafés,
to the hapless, the homeless, the hopeless, the whores,
to those bad dreams have pushed out of doors

doors open onto darkness
try this one, try that one
a handrail, a flight of steps

'Step inside,' says the man in the black bow-tie, 'Step up:
    your go –'
There's nothing but row on row
of one-armed bandits. The last of your cash: the last
    throw

throw last: is it some knack
that brings up sevens
or blind luck?

Luck has filled your pockets, and not a moment too
    soon;
luck in the shape of a hare-headed creature, adorning
the blind side of these coins which are silver like the
    moon.
You could buy your way out: be miles away by morning
and never a word of what you've heard and seen

seen but not heard
the city behind glass
not a cry, not a word

Word has it the world will end in fire and water,
word has it that love's a case of buy or barter,
word has it the final word will be 'no quarter'

quarter the city
what do you find? – the blind
leading the blind in pity

Pity those who watch from high-rise windows, pity
those who must find their shelter on the street
and the water rising . . . As for me,
I'm hare-brained, now, I'm no one you'd want to meet

meet luck with laughter
fire with water, ever
after with never never never

At the Seaside

I'm out of season, I know; the winter sun
full and low at four o'clock, a thin
wash of crimson seeping through the blue,
a sea-wind lifting twisters off the sand.
I'm what there is of me. I'm all I have in hand.

It's a place I found, but never really knew,
the perfect nowhere if you're on the run
or waiting something out. Go to the end
of the pier, to where the band-
stand is sheeted up, to where the fun-
fair has been unsprung and slackened-off,
and then go further still, a step or two,
past the Hall of Mirrors, the tented roof
of Gypsy Gina's booth, and there you stand,
as far as you meant to go and a bit beyond.

Those voices at my back might be the slap
of cleats against a mast, or else be gulls
drowning the voices out . . .
                              Open the map
and you'll see how the landline falls and fails,
how the sky lets the skyline slip
and the sea runs hard across the peaks and troughs
to pour down over the edge and become the sea,
where you yourself might yearn to go . . . a simple strip-
and-jump, feet first. Not you yourself, but me.

Deeper, it's bluer yet. A dolphin coughs
and spits a gob into the offshore tide-race
as you drift through the dusty poles and panes
of light, past the rocks, the wrecks, the reefs,

in your element, now, with the ocean's rank outsiders,
down and dirty with the bottom-feeders,
cruising the oyster bar, trawling the sea-lanes
for pick-ups, fisting mermaids back at your place . . .

The moon is up and out. The planking creaks
under the Tunnel of Love and the House of Freaks.
Not you yourself but me . . . The town
withdrawn to a sparkle of lights, the sea gone dark,
and voices, still, or the hidden music in weather.
I am waiting here for things to change their tune.
I can wait as long as it takes. I can wait for ever.

Baby Blue

She might be singing 'My buttie, my lolly, my blue-eyed
  boy'
as she stoops to take him up in joy,

then stops on a broken note, her own eyes full
as she catches a glimpse of the sky through the skull.